SMALL MAN COMPLEX

A Screenplay

Daniel Silman & Sean Freeman

ISBN: 9798434273824

CONTENTS

FOREWORD BY TOM CRUISE

This is a day off for me, because I am not shooting. I'm just chillin' now. I don't have days off.

I'm fortunate, I'm lucky. I've spent my life on movie sets and travelling the world, which is what I always wanted to do; so this is not work – I'm living the dream.

I got to actually fly in an F-14 jet which was a dream come true, and play a character I loved in Maverick.

The P-51 Mustang you see in the movie is actually my plane, so I got to pilot in those sequences. I also got to be in the jet fighter a lot more this time, which was thrilling. It was something I had been working up to.

I am very aggressive. You've got to be aggressive; there's too much responsibility not to be. When you look at Taps, a lot of that character was my childhood. I wasn't intense like that, but the character is just fear. That's what he does when he's afraid – he fights. I have an aggressive side, absolutely. I need a creative outlet. Now I work out every day. I get up and work out 45 to 60 minutes.

And that's how I start my day. Discipline is very important to me.

It's not easy. I spend a lot of time alone. I mean a lot of time alone. But I've spent time alone my whole life and it doesn't bother me. I feel lonely at times, but I don't want to get into a relationship with someone if it is not right. I'm not the type of person who just does things to do them. It takes time to get to know people.

I'm a good listener. I think it's the one characteristic that's most important. I've always been that way. Not that I take all the advice, but you've got to listen to it and have the courage to make your own decision. Then I just go for it. The important thing is to be relaxed in your work. Same in life. Don't make everything too intense. Then you can let everything go and not "act."

I hope the public and everyone realize that I'm still growing. I'm still feeling my oats here. I'm working toward the long range of what I can be as an artist. And I work my ass off trying. Because I know what I want to be.

Have you ever gotten the feeling that you aren't embarrassed yet, but you glimpse tomorrow's embarrassment?

Tom Cruise

SMALL MAN COMPLEX

10

EXT. SUBURBAN HOUSE - DAY

An average suburban house stands at the end of an average suburban street.

We drift in through the door.

INT. SUBURBAN HOUSE - HALLWAY - DAY

Photos of an average suburban family line an average suburban hallway:

We drift towards the living room.

INT. SUBURBAN HOUSE - LIVING ROOM - DAY

Average suburban furniture fills an average suburban living room:

We drift towards the arm chair...

Closer...

The arms of the chair surround us as we drift closer still...

Past a cushion...

Into the fabric of the chair itself...

And from behind a strand of fabric...

Out pops TOM MANGINER, greeting us with a wave and a tiny squeaky voice.

> TOM
> 'Ello!

DISSOLVE TO:

SMALL MAN COMPLEX

<u>5 FOOT 10 (177.8 CM)</u>

INT. BEDROOM – MORNING

JANE MANGINER, early 30s, sits in bed, going through an accounts spreadsheet on an iPad.

TOM MANGINER, 5 ft 10, Jane's husband, emerges from the en suite, dressing for work.

> TOM
> Jane, am I losing weight?
> These trousers are falling off
> me.

> JANE
> (without
> looking up)
> I'd have thought you were
> putting it on, if anything,
> dear.

Tom pulls at his waist-line. The trousers are loose.

> TOM
> Weird.

> JANE
> Tom, I think we may need to
> cancel the conservatory.
> These accounts.

Tom fixes his tie in front of the mirror.

TOM

Uh, huh. The Big Boss is
coming down today. He
wants to promote one of us
to new Chief Supervisor.

JANE

Oh, really?

TOM

Maybe I should call in
sick…

JANE

If you keep avoiding things
like this, you'll never grow
as a man.

INT. HALLWAY - MORNING

Tom stops by the children's room. Twins, DAVY & SARAH, 4
years old, are watching Youtube videos on an iPhone. Tom
struggles to get their attention.

TOM

Kids. Kids. Davy, Sarah! I'm
afraid I've got to go to work.

TWINS
(delighted)
Yaaaay.

TOM
(deflated)
You'll be in my shoes in the
blink of an eye. Let me leave
you with that thought.

                    DAVY
Your shoes are too big.

                    TOM
Not for long.

He pauses before leaving.

                    TOM
I love you, kids.

                DAVY & SARAH
Love you too, Dad.

EXT. TOM'S HOUSE - MORNING

The house sits at the corner of a suburban street.

To one side is a driveway, which leads on to the driveway of the
house behind.

Tom exits the house, pulling up his trousers at the belt.

He rounds the corner to the driveway, and the family car, a purple
Volkswagen Beatle.

In the driveway behind, neighbor HUGH JOHNSTONE, 6 ft 3 and
dressed as a cow-boy, approaches his Cadillac. He is followed by
his bleach blonde trophy wife, NANCY.

                    HUGH
Manginer! I need to borrow
your lawnmower!

                    TOM
Oh, hi, Hugh. I thought you
had my lawnmower.

                    HUGH
          I did. I sold it. I assumed
          you got a new one.

                    TOM
          I did.

                    HUGH
          I'll help myself.

Tom just stands there as Hugh and Nancy get into the Cadillac. They share a kiss and drive away.

INT. CAR - MORNING

Tom gets into the Volkswagen.

Strangely, he has to adjust the seat to reach the pedals.

Then he has to lower the rear view mirror.

He starts the engine and backs off the driveway.

EXT. BUILDING SITE - DAY

Five floors of girders stand on the cleared ground.

A rubbish chute descends from the fifth floor into a skip.

BUILDERS congregate at ground level, doing nothing. They all have beards, tattoos and muscles, having each made a concerted effort to be indistinguishable.

Their names are GARY, MARK and STEVE.

Tom approaches in the Volkswagen.

Builder, GARY, who has the largest beard, notices the car.

                    GARY
          Here's the boss. Look busy.

                    MARK
          How?

INT. CAR - MORNING

Tom drives past Gary and the builders.

                    GARY
            Morning, boss.

                    MARK
            Boss, shall I polish the
            rubbish chute again?

                    STEVE
          I'll help.

Tom drives past, uninterested.

INT. PORTACABIN - DAY

THE BIG BOSS, 7ft 2, a giant of a man in a black suit, strides
down the hallway of the cabin.

A team of six SUPERVISORS, including TOM and the determined
looking GRACE STEALS (35), flank and follow The Big Boss.

The Big Boss crouches to avoid bumping his head on the ceiling.

                    BIG BOSS
            Damn it! Who built this
            thing?

GRACE
Ex Chief Supervisor Jones,
sir.

INT. PORTACABIN - MEETING ROOM - DAY

The Big Boss sits at the head of the table.

Tom and Grace sit opposite each other amid other supervisors.

BIG BOSS
I have called you here today,
my trusted supervisors,
because this project is going
to shit!

Grace fixes her attention on The Big Boss. Other supervisors cast their eyes to the table. Tom sits blank faced.

BIG BOSS
This is where we should be.

The Big Boss clicks a palm device and the overhead projector whirs into life.

An artist's impression of a completed tower block appears on the screen.

BIG BOSS
And this is where we are.

Another click.

And the image of the building site as we know it appears - a few girders.

Another click.

An aerial view of the site.

Another click.

A long-range photo of builders, trimming each-other's beards.

> BIG BOSS
> And since this project is
> crowdfunded, with the
> scrutiny that brings, this
> could take down the whole
> damn company!

The Big Boss to his supervisors. They watch him with rapt attention, apart from Tom, who gazes out the window, at an advert which reads "Size Matters."

> BIG BOSS
> You! Is there something out
> there I'm missing?

> TOM
> Ah, no, sir.

> BIG BOSS
> Those pretty traffic lights,
> perhaps?

> TOM
> No, sir.

> BIG BOSS
> A big fluffy dinosaur waving
> its knob?

Grace bursts into sycophantic laughter.

> BIG BOSS
> You don't spot a completed
> tower block out there, do
> you?

                    TOM
      No, sir.

                  BIG BOSS
      Why not?

The Big Boss stands.

                  BIG BOSS
      Look, just because I'm 7 foot
      2, doesn't mean I don't have
      feelings.

The projector falls out of the ceiling and onto the table.

                  BIG BOSS
      Damn it, who built this
      thing?

                   GRACE
      Ex Chief Supervisor Jones,
      sir.

EXT. TOM'S HOUSE - DAY

A TROOP of high heeled feet march towards the front door.

INT. LIVING ROOM - DAY

Jane has some friends round - the high heel troop - all the same
age, weight and social status. BECKY, CLAIRE and ANNE.

A teen vampire movie plays on the TV, but the women pay no
attention. They each fixate on their phones, "checking-in" and
liking pictures on social media.

They continue to play on their phones while talking, never looking
up.

                    JANE
My husband's penis is
shrinking.

A roar of laughter.

                    BECKY
Mine's too!

                    JANE
Really, it's shrinking.

                    CLAIRE
You know what it is,
everything around them is
getting bigger, flabby gut,
flabby hips, ass - it's
just that their penises are
staying the same.

The group cackles.

                    JANE
No, it's definitely getting
smaller. I measure.

                    ANNE
Woo!

Anne spreads finger and thumb in a measurement gesture.

                    JANE
With a tape measure.

                    THE FRIENDS
Waaahaa haa haaa!

                    BECKY
When he's sleeping?

>   JUNE
> When I'm going down on
> him.

>   ANNE
> Wooo!

>   CLAIRE
> How? How?

>   JUNE
> I leave a ruler under the bed
> before doing it. I'm down
> there,
> the lights are out.

Screams of laughter.

>   JUNE
> Measurements.

June holds up a sheet of paper listing the measurements.

INT. PORTACABIN - MEETING ROOM - DAY

The meeting continues.

Tom stands awkwardly at one end of the desk. He holds the projector and points it at the screen, so that The Big Boss can continue the presentation.

>   BIG BOSS
> Now, the reason I've called
> you here, today, is that I'll be
> hosting a gathering on
> Friday night.

Click.

An image of a swanky hotel appears on the screen.

> **BIG BOSS**
> The main donors will be
> there, the board of directors.
> This is an opportunity for
> you to make amends,
> impress them, impress me.

Click.

An image of the Big Boss with Michael Jordan appears.

> **BIG BOSS**
> There's me playing
> basketball. Ignore that.

Click.

Back to the image of the hotel.

> **BIG BOSS**
> This will be your
> opportunity to impress me,
> ahead of me appointing a
> new Chief Supervisor.

The Big Boss pulls six gold envelopes from his suit pocket, each with a name on the front.

> **BIG BOSS**
> Here are your invitations...
> Smith.

Supervisor SMITH holds up his hand.

> **SMITH**
> Here, sir.

The Big Boss passes an envelope to Smith.

                    BIG BOSS
Steals.

                    GRACE
Here, sir.

                    BIG BOSS
Mangina!

                    TOM
Manginer, sir.

The meeting room erupts with laughter.

INT. PORTACABIN - DAY

Tom holds the invitation in his hand.

He looks up at a towering stationary cabinet.

A box on the top shelf, reads "For recycling."

Tom can't reach.

Grace joins Tom. In her heels, she's taller than him.

                    GRACE
Need some help?

She brings the box down for him

                    GRACE
Who put it all the way up
there?

                    TOM
I did.

> GRACE
How's that gorgeous wife of
yours?

> TOM
Oh, she's fine, Grace.
Thanks.

> GRACE
She sure is.

Tom looks at Grace, unnerved.

> GRACE
Looks like we're going to be
rivals.

There's a pause.

> GRACE
For the Chief Supervisor
position.

> TOM
Yes, right.

> GRACE
Say hi to that beautiful wife
for me.

She leaves.

Tom hesitates for a minute, and then dumps the invitation letter into the recycle box, with the other trash.

He lifts the box up to the highest shelf he can reach, the second highest from the top, and leaves it there.

INT. DINING ROOM - EVENING

Tom, Jane, Davy and Sarah sit round the dinner table.

> TOM
> How was school?

> DAVY
> We don't go to school, Dad.
> We're
> four.

> TOM
> Oh, yes.

> TWINS
> Finished.

> JANE
> Ok, then.

> SARAH
> Daddy, can you play Barbie
> with us?

> DAVY
> Play racing cars, Dad.
> Racing cars.

> TOM
> I'm very tired. You go and
> play
> together.

> SARAH
> (leaving)
> Oh, man. We hate each-
> other.

Tom and Jane are left alone. There's nothing left to say.

And then, surprisingly:

                    JANE
          Would you like some oral
          sex?

                                        FADE OUT:

<u>5 FOOT 5 (165.1 CM)</u>

INT. BEDROOM - DAY

Tom enters the bedroom from the en suit, fixing his tie.

Jane remains asleep in bed.

Tom stands in front of the mirror - which was perfectly adjusted for his height the morning before - and yet, all he can see of his own reflection is his forehead.

> TOM
> Jane, you haven't adjusted
> the mirror, have you?

Jane sleeps peacefully while her wise words from yesterday echo through the room.

> JANE (V.O.)
> If you don't take action, you
> won't grow as a man.

Tom's reflection: Worry lines appear on Tom's forehead.

> TOM
> Oh, no.

INT. HALLWAY - DAY

In the kids' bedroom, Davy swings Sarah by the hair.

> SARAH
> Ow!

Tom rushes past the room. His voice shakes.

                        TOM
              Morning kids. Bye kids.

EXT. TOM'S HOUSE - DAY

Tom bursts out of the house.

He trips over his own trousers, spins 360 degrees in the air, and lands on his ass.

INT. CAR - DAY

Unnerved and breathing heavily, Tom limps to the car.

Hugh watches from his driveway.

                        HUGH
              Morning wank?

Tom again has to adjust his seat and review mirror.

EXT. BUILDING SITE - DAY

Tom pulls up at work.

He leaves the car and heads to the portacabin with short, anxious steps.

INT. PORTACABIN - DAY

Tom stands in front of the filing cabinet.

The recycling box is where Tom left it - on the second from top shelf.

Tom can no longer reach the box.

                    TOM
         Oh, God!

Grace Steals appears at the end of the hallway.

                   GRACE
          Alright, Tom?

Tom freezes with his hands still straight up in the air.

He looks like a man caught in a hold up.

                    TOM
          Very good, thank you!

Grace eyes him suspiciously.

                    TOM
           Stretching.

EXT. BUILDING SITE - DAY

Tom exits the portacabin and dashes to the car.

He drives away.

INT. TOM'S HOUSE - DAY

Becky, Claire and Anne are on their phones. UFC is on TV.

Jane serves finger food.

                   JANE
           It's losing around an inch a
           week.

                   BECKY
          Length or girth?

JANE

Both.

CLAIRE

I tell you what you've got to
do. You should have an
affair.

JANE

Well, he's not that bad. He
just needs to man up a bit.

ANNE

Good luck with that.

The sound of Tom's car comes from outside.

JANE

He's back early.

ANNE

We'll leave you to it.

EXT. TOM'S HOUSE - DAY

Tom peers out of the car window. He looks around furtively.

He scurries to the front door and lets himself in.

INT. TOM'S HOUSE - HALLWAY - DAY

Jane and her friends greet Tom as he enters.

Tom instinctively goes up on tip toes.

JANE

Are you ok, Tom?

He sways backwards and forwards, trying to keep balance.

                    TOM
Yes. Just feeling a little light
headed.

                    BECKY
How butch.

                    JANE
The girls were just heading
out.

The women step into their high heels. They each rise ten inches in
height, and tower over Tom.

Tom responds by thrusting out his chest and extending his neck.
This strains his balance further.

                    TOM
Err...

                    CLAIRE
Oh, Jane. You know that
thing we were talking about
earlier?

                    JANE
What thing?

                    CLAIRE
The thing about your little
gardening problem.

Tom sways to and fro.

                    JANE
Oh.

                    CLAIRE
There's a number you can
call. I'll whatsapp it over.

                    JANE
I don't think that...

                    CLAIRE
Or I can IM you the contact.

Tom rocks in and out of vision between Jane and Claire.

                    TOM
Oh.

                    JANE
That really won't be
necessary.

                    BECKY
You should!

Tom collapses on the ground.

                    JANE
Tom!

                    ANNE
Are you ok?

                    TOM
I'm fine.

Anne reaches down and picks Tom up in her arms.

                    TOM
I'm really fine.

                    JANE
Take him to the sofa.

                    ANNE
He's as light as a feather.

TOM
This is unnecessary.

Anne dumps Tom onto the sofa.

JANE
Poor Tom.

Jane presses her hand against Tom's head.

BECKY
We're leaving.

CLAIRE
Sending you the number.

The women leave.

Jane remains standing over the sofa.

Tom's face glows red with embarrassment.

INT. DINING ROOM - DAY

Jane sits with the kids at dinner. Tom is absent.

DAVY
Where's Daddy?

JANE
He's in bed.

DAVY
Is he sleeping?

JANE
No.

SARAH
Is he hiding?

INT. BEDROOM -NIGHT

Tom cowers under the covers. He still wears his work clothes.

Jane enters the room wearing a night dress.

Tom shudders.

                    JANE
          Kids are asleep.

Jane gets into bed.

                    JANE
          Do you want to take your
          work clothes off? I can give
          you a massage.

                    TOM
          No thank you, Jane. I'll keep
          them on.

                    JANE
          Oh, ok. Night.

She turns off the bedside light.

INT. EN SUITE - MORNING

Tom, shaking with fear, shoves toilet tissue into his shoes.

He puts on one shoe, testing its lift.

INT. BEDROOM - DAY

Tom sneaks across the bedroom in the dark.

He takes a jacket from Jane's wardrobe and puts it on.

                    JANE
                 (sleepily)
          Why are you wearing my
          shoulder pads?

                    TOM
          Shh. You'll wake up.

He tiptoes to the door.

A stream of toilet paper trails from his shoe.

                    JANE
          Tom, your shoe. Toilet
          paper.

Jane watches the trail of toilet paper disappear out of the room.

EXT. BUILDING SITE - EQUIPMENT AREA - DAY

Safety hard-hats await collection on a rack.

Tom takes the first hat in the row.

Tom puts on the hat. It covers his eyes.

                    TOM
          Damn.

As does the second.

                    TOM
          Damn, damn.

And the third.

                    TOM
          Damn, damn, damn.

He bangs the insides of the fourth hat with a hammer.

EXT. BUILDING SITE - GROUND AREA - DAY

Tom's unit of builders stands in a row, gazing up at the
construction.

Tom approaches sheepishly.

                    TOM
          Team briefing, fellas, please.

Tom arrives at one end of the row, and notices that he's shorter
than all the other men.

He's like the bottom step in an ascending row of taller men.

                    TOM
          As you are.

Tom climbs a mud mound in front of the group.

From the mound, Tom looks down on the group. His voice shakes.

                    TOM
          Today we need to survey
          where we went wrong, how
          we can turn it around, how
          we can speed things up.

Tom puts on his elongated hat.

The builders burst into laughter.

                    TOM
          What's so funny?

                    GARY
          Nothing, boss.

                    TOM
          Exactly.

MARK
Are head penises standard
uniform, now?

Tom takes off the hat and throws it to the ground.

EXT. BUILDING SITE - VEHICLE AREA - DAY

Tom, perched in the cab of a fork lift truck, looks down on his
group of builders.

TOM
The Big Boss wants to see a
turnaround...

Tom's voice breaks into that of a chipmunk.

TOM
... and we need to figure out
how...

Tom coughs, returning his voice to normal.

TOM
And we need to figure out
how to do this.
(chipmunk)
Any ideas?

Gary puts his hand up.

TOM
Gary.

GARY
Why are you sitting up
there?

                    TOM
Let's move this to the
portacabin.

INT. PORTACABIN - MEETING ROOM - DAY

The builders, squashed into chairs, look out of place in the meeting
room.

Tom peers in through the window from his position outside.

                    TOM
Here are the site plans.

He passes sheets of paper through the window.

                    TOM
Refresh your memory.

                    MARK
Aren't you coming in?

                    TOM
Each take a copy.

                    GARY
          (half
          interested)
So, are you going for that
Chief Supervisor position,
boss, or are you gonna
chicken out?

Tom pauses at this.

                    JANE
          (v/o)
Grow as a man, grow as a
man...

INT. PORTACABIN - DAY

Tom takes the invitation from the recycling box.

The invitation glows in Tom's hands.

EXT. SWISHBANK HOTEL - NIGHT

The Volkswagen pulls up outside a glittering 5 star hotel.

INT. CAR - NIGHT

Tom and Jane admire the imposing building.

> JANE
> Tom, I'm so glad you're
> doing this.

Tom inspects the invitation in his hand.

It shines majestically.

> JANE
> If you get this promotion, we
> could afford child care. I
> could go back to work. We
> could get the conservatory
> done.

Tom let's out a deep exhale. His eyes are wide with fear.

EXT. SWISHBANK HOTEL - NIGHT

Tom and Jane exit the car.

Jane wears a beautiful blue dress and matching heels.

Tom wears a dark suit and crocodile skin boots, with lifts.

He wipes sweat from his brow.

The couple walk towards the hotel, arm in arm.

Tom twists his ankle, like he's the one in high heels.

INT. SWISHBANK HOTEL - FUNCTION ROOM - NIGHT

It's Tom's worst nightmare - a crowd of socializing strangers, trying to fill the space between them with noise.

                    TOM
          Oh, dear God.

                    JANE
          Don't be scared. You'll be
          fine.

The lights glare in Tom's eyes.

Jane tugs at his arm.

                    JANE
          Which one's your boss?

The Big Boss is surrounded by ASSISTANTS, sycophantic supervisors - including Grace Steals - and FUNDERS.

                    TOM
          There he is.

The Big Boss addresses the group.

                    BIG BOSS
I assure you that your funds
are safe with us. In fact,
here's another nominee for
the Chief Supervisor, a
change that will turn this
project around. Mangina!

                    TOM
Manginer, sir. Tom
Manginer.

Tom and Jane approach.

                    GRACE
You look ravishing, Jane.

Tom is the shortest member of the group.

                    BIG BOSS
I was just telling our funders
about the transformation
we're about to see. What are
your ideas on this, Tom?

Tom turns his head 180 degrees to an elevated podium a few
meters behind him. It rests on an enticing lifted platform.

                    BIG BOSS
Tom?

                    TOM
Transformation! Well, it's
very interesting what I have
to say...

Tom takes a step back.

                    TOM
Very interesting, indeed...

He waits while the group members, straining their necks to listen to what Tom has to say, take a collective step in his direction to get closer.

                    TOM
          I was speaking to my team
          about this today and we
          came up with some solutions
          for change which you'll want
          to hear about...

Tom takes another significant step back, and waits.

The group follows.

                    TOM
          The solutions were
          interesting and I'd like to
          share them, now.

Tom takes another step back.

                    JANE
          Tom?

She steps back to join him. The group follows.

                    TOM
          We have decided that there
          is a clear way to reverse
          direction.

Tom glances over his shoulder. He's nearly there. He thinks about it. All eyes are on him - and he steps back.

                    GRACE
          Where's he going?

The group reluctantly follows.

                    TOM
         And those solutions are...

Tom steps back and onto the podium.

He is now as tall as most members of the group.

He lets out a sigh of relief.

                    TOM
         Get ready to witness a
         significant transformation!

Through habit, he takes another step back, falls backwards off the
podium, and crashes down on a champagne trolley.

INT. DOCTOR'S OFFICE - DAY

Tom stands alongside a child's height wall chart. He is measured
by DOCTOR PARKER.

Jane sits in a chair in the corner.

                    DOCTOR
         Hmm. Very interesting? I
         think
         you'd better sit down.

Tom and the doctor take seats, the doctor beside a corner desk,
Tom beside a life sized model of the human anatomy, complete
with inflatable attachments for the breasts.

                    DOCTOR
         I must apologize for the
         decor. I share the office with
         a plastic surgeon. Try to
         ignore it.

The inflatable breasts are at Tom's head height.

> **DOCTOR**
> Fascinating contraption, isn't
> it?

> **TOM**
> Doctor, what's wrong with
> me?

> **DOCTOR**
> Well, it appears that you are
> shrinking.

> **TOM**
> Shrinking? I don't
> understand.

> **DOCTOR**
> Let me explain. Take this
> inflatable.

The doctor reaches over to the model's back and inflates the left breast to life size.

> **DOCTOR**
> Here it is, normal size, and
> now watch what happens.

He slowly lets out the air.

> **DOCTOR**
> Smaller. Slowly getting
> smaller…
> and so - are - you.

> **TOM**
> But, what, why? I don't get
> it.

> **DOCTOR**
> Let me demonstrate.

The doctor inflates the right breast to a substantial size.

                    DOCTOR
          Look at this breast. Normal
          size, would you say?

                    TOM
          Above average.

                    DOCTOR
          Slightly above average.
          Right. And watch what
          happens, now.

He deflates it.

                    DOCTOR
          Shrinking. Shrinking. And
          that is what is happening to
          you?

                    TOM
          But why me? What's going
          on? I mean, I don't
          understand.

                    DOCTOR
          You're confused.

                    TOM
          Yes, I'm confused! I mean...

                    DOCTOR
          It's fine. Look.

He inflates both breasts to a huge size. Tom has to move his head
out of the way.

                    DOCTOR
          Ok. Big, bigger. Now...

He deflates them slowly.

> DOCTOR
> Smaller, slowly getting
> smaller, shrinking, shrunk.

> TOM
> I can't believe it.

> DOCTOR
> Hmm, it is unfortunate.

> TOM
> But, did I do something to
> make this happen? Is it me?

> DOCTOR
> Entirely normal. Don't
> worry.

> TOM
> God.

> DOCTOR
> Completely natural.

> TOM
> But what do I do, now?

> DOCTOR
> Nothing. Just go about your
> daily business. Don't let it
> get to you.

> TOM
> But what's going to happen
> to me?

> DOCTOR
> Well... Shrinking, I expect.

INT. CAR - DAY

Tom gets into the driver seat. Jane gets in beside him.

They look ahead, trying to digest.

> TOM
> What do we tell the kids?

> JANE
> Tell them you're shrinking.

> DAVY
> Why are you shrinking?

The kids are in the back.

> JANE
> (looking out
> the window)
> Yes, why are you shrinking,
> Tom?

> TOM
> I don't know.

> SARAH
> What's going to happen,
> Daddy?

Jane looks at Tom. Good question.

> DAVY
> Can we still have ice cream?

> TOM
> Yeah, we can still have ice
> cream.

Tom adjusts his seat so he can reach the pedals, and starts the car.

DISSOLVE TO.

4 FOOT 9 (144.78CM)

INT. BEDROOM - MORNING

Tom hangs by his arms from the doorway to the bedroom.

Jane awakens and sees Tom's silhouette.

> JANE
>
> Tom!

> TOM
>
> Morning, Jane!

> JANE
>
> Tom! I thought you'd hung
> yourself.

> TOM
>
> I'm just stretching.

> JANE
>
> Jesus!

> TOM
>
> Hung myself? It's not that
> bad!

Davy and Sarah push Tom's legs aside and run into the room.

> DAVY
>
> Mum, can we go to the toy
> shop?

> JANE
>
> I don't know, kids. The
> budget...

                              TOM
I can take them.

                              JANE
Aren't you going to work?

                              TOM
I'm shrinking.

                              JANE
So, you're just going to hang
around here, are you? Like
that's going to make me
respect you more.

Pause.

                              TOM
Can you help me down?

INT. CAR - DAY

Tom sits on an elevated cushion. He steers the car into the building
site.

Up ahead, the newly promoted Grace Steals, dressed in a power
suit, points orders to her growing team.

Tom shakes his head and does a u-turn.

EXT. THE MORNING SUN BAR - DAY

Tom pulls up in the car outside a 24 hour bar.

INT. THE MORNING SUN BAR - DAY

Tom enters.

The BARMAN cleans a glass in front of the sole other customer, a man with his back turned to us at the bar.

Tom approaches.

He climbs up onto the bar stool - literally climbs.

                    TOM
          I'll have a beer.

                    BARMAN
          Got any ID?

Tom climbs back down.

The fellow customer looks up. It's grizzled EX CHIEF SUPERVISOR JONES.

                    JONES
          It's ok. He's with me.

                    TOM
          Chief Supervisor Jones!

                    JONES
          He's of age.

Tom climbs back up the stool.

                    JONES
          He just appears to be
          shrinking.

The Barman serves a beer.

                    TOM
          I haven't seen you, since...

JONES
I got laid off... Don't worry,
you can say it. I've been
getting my life in order.

TOM
Where have you been?

JONES
Here. It's ok, I deserved it. I
stopped trying. I let things
slip. How are things with
you?

TOM
I'm shrinking.

JONES
Damn! That is mighty
unfortunate.

TOM
Yeah.

JONES
What are you gonna do
about it?

TOM
I don't know. The doctor
said I'm just going to keep
shrinking...

JONES
Yeah, but what are you
going to do to make it
better? Look at me. Do you
think my life has got better,
me just sitting here,
drinking?

TOM

No.

JONES

No. It sure feels better, but it 'aint got better.

TOM

I'm worried everyone's gonna laugh at me.

JONES

Look, a man can either shape his own world, or let it shape him. You don't want them to laugh at you, you don't let them laugh at you.

TOM

How?

JONES

You take action. You go out there and you become so damn impressive that they 'aint gonna laugh at you; they gonna look up to you.

TOM

I can do that?

JONES

You can do that.

TOM

I'm going to change. I'm going to shape my own world.

He hops off the stool and skips to the door.

>   TOM
>   Thanks for the beer.

>   JONES
>   I 'aint paying.

The Barman cocks a rifle.

Open montage music: "Mission Impossible" theme.

INT. CLOTHING STORE - DAY

Tom stands in front of a dressing mirror, wearing sunglasses.

He puts a second pair of glasses - aviators - over his sunglasses.

In slow motion, he puts on a leather jacket.

INT. BARBERSHOP - DAY

The BARBER blow dries Tom's hair into an inflated quiff.

>   TOM
>   Bigger. Bigger.

INT. SHOE SHOP - DAY

Tom pulls on a pair of high heeled cowboy boots. The shop assistant backs away, giving Tom enough space to get a feel for the boots.

>   TOM
>   Higher.

EXT. TATTOO PARLOR - DAY

The sound of electronic needles and screaming comes from inside a seedy looking tattoo joint.

INT. TATTOO PARLOR - MAIN ROOM - DAY

CUSTOMERS have their limbs tattooed by tattoo ARTISTS.

The screaming continues, coming from a back room.

INT. TATTOO PARLOR - BACK ROOM - DAY

Tom continues to scream as a tattoo artist rubs on the final lines of a skull and crossbones impermanent tattoo.

                    TOM
          Phew.

                    TATTOO ARTIST
          All done.

                    TOM
          How long will it last?

                    TATTOO ARTIST
          Around a day.

                    TOM
          Cool.

                    TATTOO ARTIST
          Did you want the bubble
          gum?

The tattoo artist holds up the bubble gum pack - included with the free stick-on tattoo.

                    TOM
        Hit me.

INT. TANNING SALON - DAY

Tom steps into a tanning booth. He keeps his sunglasses on.

Fake tan sprays at Tom from all angles.

EXT. BUILDING SITE - GROUND AREA - DAY

The builder group, Gary, Mark and Steve, stand around comparing
biceps.

Tom pulls up in the purple Volkswagen.

A giant eagle sticker is plastered on the hood, like that of a T-Bird.

Tom gets out of the car and strikes a Superman pose, hands on
hips, chest thrust forward.

He wears tight, ball hugging jeans, the leather jacket, elevated
cowboy boots, bouffant, streaked hair, fake tan and aviator glasses.

                                        END MONTAGE

Tom strides over to his team.

                    TOM
        I know I'm late. I had to kick
        some guy's ass on the way
        over.

                    GARY
        Who's ass?

                    TOM
        Ex military. Deserter.

GARY

You kicked his ass?

TOM

Woo!

MARK

That's cool, bro.

TOM

Then I had some sex.

GARY

Just now?

TOM

Woo!

GARY

Who did you have sex with?

TOM

Who didn't I have sex with?

MARK

There was more than one?

GARY

It was an orgy?

MARK

It's not even lunch time yet.

TOM

Woo! That's how it is, fellas.
That's how it is.

Grace Steals appears at the side.

                    GRACE
          Tom. May I speak with you
          and your team, inside?

INT. LIVING ROOM - DAY

Jane is having another get-together with her friends, Becky, Claire
and Anne. The stench of empathy is in the air.

Jane has been crying.

                    BECKY
          It's typical of them, isn't it?

                    CLAIRE
          Don't you worry. Don't you
          worry.

                    JANE
          I've given him everything,
          you know? Marriage,
          children...

                    CLAIRE
          I know, I know.

                    BECKY
          And then he decides to start
          shrinking.

                    CLAIRE
          The bastard.

                    JANE
          I know it's not his fault,
          but...

                    BECKY
Don't start making excuses
for him, Jane. You're the
victim, here.

                    CLAIRE
Come here.

Claire gives Jane a hug, loving it.

INT. PORTACABIN - MEETING ROOM - DAY

Grace stands in front of the seated builders.

Tom stands with one leg on a chair, his leather jacket tossed over
his shoulder.

                    GRACE
Won't you sit down, Tom?

                    TOM
I'm cool.

                    GRACE
There have been complaints
about noise levels and
completion dates. We need
to produce a freebie to go
out to the community.

                    GARY
How about a calendar?

                    GRACE
A topless builder theme!

                    GARY
It'll be a right laugh!

                    MARK
Yeah!

                    TOM
YEAH!

                    GRACE
You like that idea Tom?

                    TOM
YEAH!

                    GRACE
You can go on the cover.

                    TOM
YEAH!

INT. BATHROOM - DAY

Tom draws "abs" on his stomach with a marker.

                    TOM
          Come and get me, Grace. I'll
          be ready.

INT. LIVING ROOM - DAY

Claire and Anne sit with Jane. Becky returns from the front door, with CHAD, a filthy, shaven headed sub-moron in a wife-beater t-shirt, and sporting a number of piercings.

                    BECKY
              (to Jane)
This is Chad. He's self
employed, very independent;
he cleans bathrooms.
              (to Chad)
Isn't that right, Chad?

                    CHAD
'Suppose.

                    CLAIRE
It's not easy to find a man
who can keep the bathroom
clean.

Laughter.

                    ANNE
Wooo.

                    BECKY
But he wants to become a
pool
cleaner, don't you Chad?

                    CHAD
'Suppose. Yeah.

                    CLAIRE
You've got some lovely
piercings
there, Chad. What are they?

                    CHAD
Piercings.

Awkward silence.

                    CLAIRE
Yes, well...

                    CHAD
Um, which one of yous is I
gonna screw?

                    JANE
Oh, Jesus.

                    CHAD
It's free, right?

                    BECKY
Um.

                    CHAD
Coz I's got this shitter to
clean that's covered in the
stuff.

EXT. BUILDING SITE - GROUND AREA - DAY

Tom stands in front of his builders, addressing the group.

He now adopts a croaky voice.

                    TOM
Guys, gather round. There's
something I have to say.

He points at them, maintaining eye contact.

                    TOM
I like you guys.

                    GARY
We like you, too, boss.

                    TOM
You didn't have to say that.

                    MARK
We mean it.

                    TOM
You didn't have to.
          (choked up)
Let's blow this joint!

                    GARY
What's that boss.

                    TOM
Let's head home early. I like
you. Let's roll!

Tom trots off to his car.

The group follows to the car park, removing their hats.

A PHOTOGRAPHER chases after them but the group escapes.

                    PHOTOGRAPHER
Wait, your calendar.

INT. CAR - DAY

Tom drives home. Indie music on the radio.

Tom changes to the channel. It's Bruce Springsteen.

                    BRUCE SPRINGSTEEN
Born in the USA!
Born in the USA!

                    TOM
Yeah!

He turns up the volume, liking it.

But the station loses its signal, so he switches to:

> KENNY LOGGINS
>> Highway to the Danger
>> Zone,
>> Ride into the Danger Zone.

> TOM
>> Ha!

Tom winds down the window, rests his arm on the door and lets the wind further inflate his hair.

Tom changes the channel.

> EMINEM
>> You've gotta,
>> Lose yourself,
>> In the music,
>> You gotta…

> TOM
>> Yes!

He speeds up.

INT. LIVING ROOM - DAY

The weep-a-thon continues.

> BECKY
>> If an affairs not the answer,
>> I'll tell you what you do.
>> Leave him.

> CLAIRE
>> Yes.

                    BECKY
          That'll teach him.

The car pulls up outside. The radio blares out a Herman the Tosser
rap, full blast.

               HERMAN THE TOSSER
          You gotta,
          Blow,
          Shit,
          Blow that up.

                    CLAIRE
          I like that song.

                    JANE
          Neighbors.

The car music stops.

                    BECKY
          How about you come out
          with us
          tonight? The four of us.

EXT. TOM'S HOUSE - DAY

Tom gets out of the car.

Davy and Sarah shuffle around in a tent on the front lawn.

                    TOM
          Kids. Are you coming in
          with me?

                    DAVY
          No.

                    SARAH
          You're scary.

INT. LIVING ROOM - DAY

Tom enters.

                    TOM
          Hello, ladies.

He kisses Jane on the head, passing through and out of the living room.

The friends were not expecting his appearance.

INT. BEDROOM - DAY

Tom dumps his work folders on the bed, looks at himself in the mirror and loosens his collar.

INT. LIVING ROOM - DAY

The friends talk in hushed tones.

                    BECKY
          He doesn't care how you
          feel. You can tell. He just
          comes in here...

Tom enters, whistling. He picks up a newspaper and slumps into an armchair. He starts to read.

Tom looks up, over the newspaper.

Four pairs of scowling, confused, hateful eyes aim his way.

                    TOM
          I'm gonna go out to the
          garden and take up mixed
          martial arts.

EXT. GARDEN - DAY

Tom stretches slowly and then erupts into some mid-air chops.

The garden behind his, separated by a fence, belongs to neighbor
Hugh.

Hugh and his trophy girlfriend sit on their porch, drinking wine,
watching the strange show performed by Tom.

                    HUGH
          He's just such an easy target.
          I love it.

INT. KITCHEN - DAY

Jane looks out of the window at Tom.

Tom performs a series of chops, kicks and punches. He screams
out aggressively with each action.

Becky joins Jane at her side.

                    BECKY
          I think it's obvious what
          you're gonna have to do.
          You're going to have to kill
          him.

                    JANE
               (sadly)
          Please leave.

Becky looks at Jane, slightly taken aback. She backs away.

Jane looks out of the window as Tom performs a roundhouse hick and falls on his ass.

DISSOLVE TO:

<u>3 FOOT 11 (119.38CM)</u>

INT. BEDROOM - MORNING

Morning light streams through the cracks in the curtains, just enough to guide Tom out of bed and across the bedroom.

Jane sleeps on.

Tom reaches for the light switch. He can't reach it.

> TOM
>
> What the...?

Tom goes to the mirror - adjusted for height on the wall.

Tom is now the size of an average seven year old.

> TOM
> (startled)
> Oh for...
> (panic)
> Oh come on.

Moments later:

Tom paces the bedroom, clutching his hair, anxiously.

Moments later:

Tom does press ups at the foot of the bed.

Moments later:

Tom, back in front of the mirror, performs bicep curls with dumb bells.

> TOM
> That's it. That's it.

                    JANE
              (sleepily)
Mmmph. What are you
doing with my lady weights?

                    TOM
              (panting)
I just thought I'd take up a
bit of exercise.

                    JANE
Why don't you go for a
walk?

EXT. TOM'S HOUSE - MORNING

Tom paces up and down outside the front of the house, with
nervous, short, steps.

He catches himself in the wing mirror of a car, tip-toeing to see the
top of his head.

Tom returns to walking, this time swinging his arms behind him as
he walks.

Tom stops and turns. He walks back, arms swinging behind, now
with legs wider apart.

INT. HOUSE - MORNING

Jane and the twins look out the window at Tom.

                    SARAH
What's he doing, Mummy?

                    JANE
I don't know, Sarah.

Arms still swinging, legs bowed, Tom walks with rolling shoulders, like he's on a ship at high seas.

> JANE
> He seems to be developing a
> strut.

EXT. HOUSE - DAY

In addition to the new array of hideous movements, Tom now flicks his head as he walks.

Jane appears at the front door.

> JANE
> Tom. Why don't you take the
> kids to the toy store?

Tom puffs out his cheeks.

> JANE
> Thinking of an excuse?

> TOM
> I'm trying.

> JANE
> Don't overspend.

INT. CAR - DAY

Tom has blocks of wood tied to his feet so he can reach the peddles. He sits on a Dora the Explorer cushion.

Still, he can barely see over the steering wheel.

The car passes a play park.

> DAVY

Park!

> SARAH

Can we go to the park,
Daddy?

> TOM

Will you throw a tantrum if
we don't?

> DAVY

I expect we will, yes.

INT. KITCHEN - DAY

Jane sits at the breakfast table with her laptop open.

She scrolls through an expenses spreadsheet, head in hands.

Her mobile rings.

> JANE
> (into phone)

Hello.

> GRACE
> (over phone)

Jane! Grace. I was just
calling to see if Tom was
coming in.

> JANE

Today? I didn't think he was
due in, today.

GRACE
Yes, we're working overtime
until project completion.
Tom knows that.

JANE
He's been having some
issues. I'll ask Tom to speak
to you about that.

GRACE
(laughing)
That's what it's like dealing
with a man. Always let you
down.

JANE
Ah.

GRACE
(laughing)
Women, however. Women
deliver.

JANE
Right.

GRACE
And how are you doing,
Jane, dear? Still hoping for
the conservatory?

JANE
Oh, that's on hold. I'm trying
to figure out how to make
ends meet.

GRACE
You shouldn't give up on
your dreams. Fantasies...

                    JANE
          I'd like to be able to sit out
          there, with Tom, watching
          the kids.

                    GRACE
          I could do that building
          work for you. It'd be good to
          get my overalls on again. Or
          off again, for that matter.

Jane laughs nervously.

EXT. PARK - DAY

The twins play on a climbing frame. Tom looks at his watch -
bored as hell.

                    DAVY
          Dad, can you play with us?

Tom screws up his face.

                    SARAH
          Come on Daddy. Why not?

She has a point.

Tom looks left and right. There's nobody around.

Kenny Loggins' "Danger Zone" kicks in.

Tom, on the monkey bars, swings ably.

He makes it all the way across.

                    DAVY & SARAH
          Yaay!

Tom takes a bow.

Danger Zone.

Two 30 something mothers, pushing prams, enter the park, TRINA and LUCY.

Tom, Davy and Sarah, on swings, compete to go higher.

> TOM/TWINS
> Weee!

Trina and Lucy breastfeed on the park bench.

> TRINA
> It's lovely seeing them play
> together, isn't it?

Danger Zone.

Tom goes head first down the slide.

> TOM
> Shiiiit!

Danger Zone.

> LUCY
> That older one's a bit over
> zealous.

> TOM
> There's a big shiny slide like
> this at Daddy's work. Gotta
> try it out!

> DAVY
> Can we?

Tom and the twins spin on the round-a-bout.

Tom staggers off and vomits.

TOM
Hell, yeah!

Danger Zone.

Trina and Lucy approach Tom, as he goes mental on the seesaw.

TRINA
Excuse me, little boy. Little
boy.

TOM
What did you call me?

TRINA & LUCY
(realizing)
Oh.
(repulsed)
Oh.

INT. CAR. DAY

Tom speeds away from the park.

SARAH
Why are we leaving?

DAVY
Is it because that lady called
you a little boy?

TOM
No.

SARAH
You're not a little boy.

                    TOM
Thank you, Sarah.

                   SARAH
You're a little man.

They stop at a traffic light.

Tom catches a reflection of himself in the wing mirror.

                    TOM
Sarah, take my phone. Take
a photo of me for Instagram.

Tom hands her the phone.

                   SARAH
You don't have an Instagram
feed.

                    TOM
I'm getting one. Take one of
me driving and looking cool.

                   SARAH
But we're stopped.

                    TOM
I'll pretend.

He strikes a pose with one arm resting out the window and hair
tossed back.

Sarah takes photos.

                    TOM
No, take it from a low angle.

                   SARAH
I can't get much lower.

                    TOM
          Looking up at me.

                    DAVY
          He wants you to get on the
          floor.

A 4x4 full of college STUDENTS pulls up beside the car.

The students spot Tom immediately and burst into laughter.

                    MALE STUDENT
          Look, a leprechaun driving a
          car.

                    FEMALE STUDENT
          Excuse me, why is your
          steering wheel so big?

Tom winds up the window, to no avail.

                    TOM
          This car!

                    MALE STUDENT
          Is this the right way to
          munchkin land?

The lights change and the 4x4 drives off.

Sarah photographs Tom struggling with the window.

EXT. TOY SHOP - DAY

The kids lead Tom to the shop.

He looks up at the sign: "Little People."

                    TOM
         Oh, God.

INT. TOY STORE - DAY

Davy plays in a ball pen.

Sarah looks at Barbies.

Tom comes over.

                    TOM
          Come on. Just choose one.

                    SARAH
          They're all so pretty.

                    TOM
          Just choose your favorite.
          Come on.

                    SARAH
          Blonde Barbie. I like her.

                    TOM
          Yeah, she's not bad.

A frumpy store assistant, HEIDI, joins them, listening-in with a
smile.

                    SARAH
          But...

Sarah pulls blonde Barbie off the shelf to reveal... Hip-hop Barbie.
An absolute stunner, with streaked brown Latina hair.

Tom grabs her off the shelf.

TOM
Yes, get this one.

HEIDI
Need any help?

Sarah takes a red headed Barbie.

SARAH
But this one's a gymnast.

TOM
That's important, but I don't
know. It's so difficult to
decide. Oh look!

He takes a black Barbie down and weighs her up with Hip-Hop
Barbie. Black Barbie is wearing hot-pants.

SARAH
Roller-Barbie.

TOM
Is she? So difficult to
choose.

SARAH
I think I'll get gymnast
Barbie.

TOM
No, don't get gymnast
Barbie.

SARAH
But she's my favorite.

TOM
You've just met her.

                    HEIDI
          Why don't you let the girl,
          choose?

Tom's voice breaks into chipmunk at the worst moment.

                    TOM
          Back off, lady.

                    HEIDI
          That's it. Where are your
          parents?

Tom affects a deep voice, like Batman:

                    TOM
          My parents have been dead
          for ten years.

EXT. TOY STORE - DAY

Tom drags the kids, carrying bags of shopping.

                    DAVY
          Where are we going?

                    TOM
          Come on.

The kids jump in the car.

Tom opens the boot and dumps in the shopping. He's bought every
Barbie in the store.

EXT. CIGAR STORE - DAY

The car pulls up outside a cigarette shop.

Tom gets out.

The kids wait in the car.

INT. CAR - DAY

Davy and Sarah watch Tom as he hovers outside the store.

> SARAH
> What's he doing?

> DAVY
> I think he's taking up
> smoking.

Tom stops a group of BMX KIDS on their bikes.

They exchange words, and Tom hands over cash to the tallest of the kids.

The tall kid enters the store, while Tom waits nervously with the other kids.

Sarah takes photos on Tom's phone.

> SARAH
> Daddy's Instagram.

The tall kid exits.

He hands Tom a pack of cigars.

Tom shakes his hand, and quickly returns and gets in the car.

> TOM
> Lucky we got served.

> DAVY
> Where now, Dad?

> TOM
> The dog pound.

                    SARAH
We're getting a puppy!

                    TOM
No, we're getting a dog

                    DAVY
This is fun!

INT. KENNEL - DAY

A DOG CARER leads Tom, Davy and Sarah through the kennel.

                    TOM
           I want something with
           status. A bulldog, rottweiler,
           pit-bull.

                    DOG CARER
           Those dogs are notoriously
           difficult to look after, sir.
           You have to be very, um,
           physical.

                    TOM
           I'm physical.

                    DOG CARER
           How about this one? This
           one may be more suitable.

The dog carer points at a small poodle.

Tom points to a pit-bull.

                    TOM
           This is my dog.

EXT. CAR SHOWROOM - DAY

The family car pulls up outside the showroom.

INT. CAR SHOWROOM - DAY

Tom walks into the showroom.

He stands, hands on hips, feet apart, like a superhero.

                    TOM
              (as Batman)
           Give me the fastest thing
           you've got... On a part
           exchange pay plan.

EXT - CAR SHOWROOM - DAY

The twins wait by the car lot with their bags of toys, and the pitbull, with it's studded collar.

Tom screeches to a halt in front of them in a red, two-seater, tiny
open top sports car.

He takes off his sunglasses.

                    TOM
           Which of you is going to
           walk?

                    SARAH
           We could share the
           passenger seat.

                    TOM
           Deal.

Tom and the twins speed off in the car. Its number plate is
BIGMAN.

INT. LIVING ROOM - DAY

Newspapers line the coffee table - classified job ads with circles around certain jobs.

Jane looks at an old photo of herself, Tom and the twins.

A car pulls up in the driveway blasting out hip-hop.

EXT. HOUSE - DAY

Jane opens the front door and steps out.

The twins get out of the sports car and run with their bags of toys into the house.

                    TWINS
          Hi Mum.

Tom gets out of the car in slow motion. He is covered in jewelry, metallic studs and chains on his leather jacket. He leans against the car and lights a cigar.

Jane compares the Tom of the photo in her hand to the newly arrived Tom. Unrecognizable.

Tom opens the car door again and lets out the pit-bull dog. A lead is tied to its studded collar.

He struts, with the dog, towards Jane.

                    TOM
              (Batman)
          Hey baby.

The dog runs off down the street, pulling Tom with it.

                    TOM
                (Chipmunk)
        Help.

Jane watches her husband dragged away into the distance by the
dog.

INT. LIVING ROOM - DINING TABLE - DAY

Tom, Jane, Davy and Sarah sit at the dining table. Tom is
scratched and bruised.

Beside him, sits the poodle from the kennel, wearing a studded
collar.

The kids eat with their hands.

                    TOM
            Since when did the kids eat
            with their hands?

                    JANE
            Well, you haven't been
            giving them much attention,
            lately. How was your trip?

                    DAVY
            Dad joined a biker gang.

                    JANE
        Oh, did he?

                    TOM
            I'm going to need to buy a
            BMX.

The kids finish their food.

                    SARAH
All done!

They leave the room.

Tom and Jane sit in silence.

                    JANE
          So...

                    TOM
          How about some oral sex?

                    JANE
          Screw you.

INT. PORTACABIN - MEETING ROOM - DAY

Tom sits across from Grace Steals and, to her right, an
employment lawyer, MS. TOADY.

Steals unfolds a doctor's note on the desk in front of her. She and
Toady eye Tom suspiciously. It's awkward.

                    GRACE
          This is Ms. Toady. She's an
          employment lawyer who I've
          called in to accompany me
          today.

                    TOM
          Hello.

                    GRACE
          Apparently, there are no
          legal grounds to dismiss
          someone on account of...

TOM
That is good news.

GRACE
Well, on behalf of the
company I must offer my
condolences.

MS. TOADY
Condolences.

GRACE
This note from your doctor
seems to suggest that you
are becoming - increasingly
diminutive.

MS. TOADY
Littler.

GRACE
It then goes on to say
something, apparently, about
prosthetic breasts, which I
neither do, nor want to
understand.

MS. TOADY
Breasts.

Grace scrutinizes a word on the note.

GRACE
Murderers?

MS. TOADY
Mammaries.

                    GRACE
But aside from all this,
there's something about you
Tom. I sense a certain, if not
insubordination, an
absenteeism.

                    TOM
Oh?

                    GRACE
And this is just the latest in a
long line...

                    MS. TOADY
Deliberate.

                    GRACE
I don't tolerate shrinking
from my staff, do you
understand? And
it's not something I'm going
to tolerate from you.

                    TOM
No.

                    GRACE
This note seems to
recommend you have some
compassionate, or sick
leave to deal with whatever
it is you're doing, for an
indefinite period of time.

                    MS. TOADY
Indefinite.

                    GRACE
You've got two weeks.

                    TOM
    Right.

                    GRACE
    Oh, and Tom, when you
    come back, lose the stilts.
    They're a health hazard on a
    building site.

                    TOM
    What stilts?

EXT. BUILDING SITE - GROUND AREA - DAY

The builders, Gary, Mark and Steve, stand around.

Tom strides past them on stilts.

The stilts, tucked under his jeans, give him a height of 7 foot 2.

Tom wobbles swinging each leg into the air with each step.

The whole building site stops to watch the spectacle.

Tom steps into some uneven ground and loses his balance.

The fall seems to take an age, but when Tom finally crashes into the ground, he does so with his face slamming into mud.

The builders rush to his aid.

                    GARY
    Are you all right?

They turn him over.

Tom coughs up mud.

Builders on girders, in vehicles, standing around, all point and laugh.

MARK
Let's get these off you.

They try to drag the stilts out of his trousers, but this merely pulls
Tom along with the force.

TOM
Aarrgh.

GARY
Hold him down.

Some of the group hold Tom down, while Gary and Mark pull at a
stilt each - pulling and shaking Tom's legs.

TOM
Aarrgh.

MARK
Push. Push.

The onlooking builders stop laughing now. They're witnessing a
birth, a miracle.

GARY
It's coming. It's coming.

TOM
Aarrgh.

He's free!

Gary and Mark fall back onto the mud, each clutching a stilt.

The building site erupts into cheers.

Tom scrambles to his feet, and charges to his sports car.

TOM
Aarrgh.

Grace, hands on hips, watches as Tom drives away.

                    GRACE
          Men.

INT. THE MORNING SUN BAR - DAY

Tom enters. He is covered in mud and wildly disheveled.

He limps over to the bar, and climbs onto the stool beside Ex Chief
Supervisor Jones.

The barman serves Tom a beer.

Jones doesn't even look up.

                    JONES
          I never said it'd be easy.

Suddenly, Gary, Mark, the rest of the building group enter the bar,
and take seats at tables.

                    GARY
          Lunch time!

Tom sinks his head, not wanting to be seen.

The place fills up fast.

Tom turns to Jones. His voice is full chipmunk now, with an added
wheeze.

                    TOM
              (singing)
          I'm the kid that's all the
          candy,
          I'm a Yankee Doodle Dandy,
          I'm glad I am.

JONES
So's Uncle Sam.

Tom hops up onto the bar stool and faces the crowd.

TOM
(singing)
I'm a real live Yankee
Doodle,
Made my name and fame
and boodle,
Just like Mister Doodle did,
by riding on a pony.
I love to listen to the Dixie
strain;
"I long to see the girl I left
behind me!"
And that ain't a josh, She's a
Yankee, by gosh.

BARMAN
(singing)
Oh, say can you see.

Tom hops up onto the bar.

TOM
(singing)
Anything about a Yankee
that's a phoney
(dancing)
I'm a Yankee Doodle Dandy,
A Yankee Doodle, do or die;
A real live nephew of my
Uncle Sam's,
Born on the Fourth of July.
I've got a Yankee Doodle
sweetheart,

She's my Yankee Doodle
joy.

Tom hops down from the bar and begins to walk among the tabled
crowd.

GARY AND MARK
(singing)
Yankee Doodle came to
London,
Just to ride the ponies;
He is the Yankee Doodle
Boy.

Tom climbs up onto the table of Gary, Mark and the team, and
addresses the crowd.

TOM
(singing)
Father's name was Hezikiah,
Mother's name was Ann
Maria,
Yanks through and through.
Red, White and Blue,
Father was so Yankee
hearted,
When the Spanish war was
started,
He slipped in his uniform
and hopped upon a pony.
My mother's mother was a
Yankee free,
My father's father was a
Yankee too;
And that's going some,
For the Yankees by gosh,
Oh, say can you see
Any thing about my
pedigree that's phoney?

Tom leaps down from the table and performs what may be described as a dance, imitating James Cagney's movement when performing the same song.

He marches back and forth, strange and hyper-gnome like.

He bandies his legs around so that they look like rubber.

Then he runs and bounces off a wall.

Meanwhile, everyone in the bar erupts into a chorus.

                    EVERYONE
                 (singing)
           He's a Yankee Doodle
           Dandy,
           A Yankee Doodle, do or die;
           A real live nephew of his
           Uncle Sam's,
           Born on the Fourth of July.
           He's got a Yankee Doodle
           sweetheart,
           She's his Yankee Doodle
           joy.

                    TOM
                 (singing)
           Yankee Doodle came to
           London,
           Just to ride the ponies;
           I am the Yankee Doodle
           Boy.

And he marches out the bar.

INT. BEDROOM - DAY

Tom awakes from a horrific dream.

He breathes heavily.

Calming himself down, he shakes his head.

                    TOM
          What was all that about?

Then he spots them: upright in the corner - the stilts.

                    TOM
          Oh, God.

He sinks back down into bed.

                              DISSOLVE TO.

2 FOOT 2 (66CM)

INT. BEDROOM - MORNING

It's still dark in the room.

The twilight streams through the cracks in the curtains, barely enough to guide Tom out of bed and across the bedroom, while Jane sleeps softly.

                         TOM
              What the...?

Tom opens the curtains, enough to let the light through, and goes to the mirror.

Tom is now the size of a two year old.

                         TOM
              Oh for...
                    (panic)
              Oh come on.

MOMENTS LATER:

Tom paces the bedroom. He clutches his hair in exasperation and anxiety.

MOMENTS LATER:

Tom does press-ups at the foot of the bed.

MOMENTS LATER:

Tom, back in front of the mirror, performs star jumps.

> JANE

Outside!

EXT. BACK GARDEN - DAY

Tom performs yoga stretches on the garden lawn.

He bends over backwards, balancing on his hands, and sticks one leg in the air.

Hugh appears at the fence which partitions the gardens of his and Tom's house.

> HUGH

Morning, Tom.

Tom is at full stretch and can hardly speak.

> TOM

Hugh.

> HUGH

Don't mind me.

Hugh begins to dig up the garden fence, uprooting the partition in sections and, moving it towards Tom's house, where he plants it.

Tom falls out of his position and sits on the ground.

> TOM

What are you doing?

> HUGH

I'm extending our garden.
The little lady inside said
she wanted ours bigger.

Tom gets to his feet, and Hugh pauses.

                    TOM
Oh.

                    HUGH
Well, what are you waiting
for? A'int ya going to help
me?

INT. KITCHEN - DAY

Jane prepares cereal for Davy and Sarah as they hover nearby.

                    SARAH
Mummy, I had a dream
about Daddy and he got
squashed...

The door bell rings.

Jane hands the cereal to the children.

                    JANE
Here kids, go and eat at the
table.

Jane answers the door as the kids go to the dining room.

It's Grace in her power suit and high heels.

                    GRACE
Jane, I wanted to talk to you
personally about why I had
to suspend Tom from his
job.

                    JANE
Suspend?

                    GRACE
Oh! He hasn't told you, has
he?

                    JANE
No.

                    GRACE
They never do. May I come
in?

Jane nods.

Grace follows Jane into the kitchen.

Jane positions herself on a stool, and Grace stands up close next to
her.

                    GRACE
I want to keep this
professional, but as a friend,
I need to ask, can I touch
your boobs?

                    JANE
Pardon me?

                    GRACE
To compare them. We can
compare boobs and then see
what happens.

EXT. GARDEN - DAY

Hugh continues to move parts of the fence towards Tom's house,
extending his own garden and shortening Tom's.

Tom walks tentatively up to his repositioned fence.

He clears his throat.

TOM

Um... I 'm not sure I like you
doing that.

Hugh stops what he's doing, drops his tools and walks up to Tom,
the fence being the only thing keeping them apart.

HUGH

You're not sure, or you're
sure you don't like me doing
that?

TOM

I'm... I'm sure.

HUGH

Well, tell me, Manginer.
What are you going to do
about it?

Tom clears his throat. He dangles his arms by his side and let's
them swing to and fro an inch.

He nods his head.

Then Tom turns around and goes inside.

INT. KITCHEN - DAY

Grace stands over Jane, leaning in.

JANE

I think you've
misunderstood.

                    GRACE
        I'm sorry. Sorry. What I
        meant to say was...
                    (singing)
        You are so beautiful, to me,
        Can't you see.
        You are so beautiful, to me...

The sound of Tom entering is heard off screen.

                    TOM (O/S)
        Honey, do we have a tape
        measure?

                    JANE
        What?

                    TOM (O/S)
        For the garden.

                    JANE
        There's one under the bed.

Tom enters the kitchen.

                    TOM
        What's it doing under the
        bed?

Tom sees Grace leaning in over Jane.

                    TOM
        What's going on?

                    GRACE
        We were just going to make
        love.

                    TOM
        What?

                    JANE
No, we weren't!

                    GRACE
We were going to touch
boobs and...

                    TOM
I don't believe this!

He picks up a bowl of fruit and throws it at the wall. Fruit scatters
across the floor.

                    JANE
Tom.

                    TOM
I've had enough of this! The
neighbor is taking over my
garden. My boss is making
moves on my wife!

He stamps on an orange, but his tiny foot merely bounces back up.
Repeatedly.

                    JANE
What are you doing?

                    TOM
Aaaargh!

                    GRACE
He's trying to crush them!

                    JANE
You can't crush them!

                    TOM
I will crush them.

                    JANE
        Stop it, Tom. You'll hurt
        yourself!

                    GRACE
        He will hurt himself.

                    TOM
            (to Grace)
        You get out. Out. Out.

Grace leaves.

Tom stamps on an orange one more time.

                    TOM
        I will crush them later!

He leaves the kitchen.

INT. BEDROOM - DAY

Tom stomps to and fro in his bedroom, raging with hurt pride.

                    TOM
        How dare they? How dare
        they? I won't let them get
        away with this.

Tom goes to the wardrobe.

He takes the shoulder pads from Jane's jacket.

                    TOM
        They'll be sorry.

INT. KIDS BEDROOM - DAY

Tom takes a small blue jacket from Davy's wardrobe.

He pulls some fake medals off of a soldier teddy bear.

He takes a summer hat from a teddy bear and bends the rim.

He looks in the mirror.

He's Napoleon.

EXT. BUILDING SITE - GROUND AREA - DAY

Gary, Mark and co, polish the metallic garbage chute leading from the building.

> MARK
> You going down the tanning
> place?

> GARY
> Yeah, later.

> STEVE
> I will.

They take a step back and survey their work with a sigh.

> MARK
> What did she mean, look
> busy?

> TOM (O/S)
> Enough of this nonsense!

The men stop what they're doing and turn to see Tom.

He's dressed as Napoleon, standing on a box with his arms behind his back.

TOM
Men, no longer will we be
given menial tasks, just to
look busy.

GARY
What do you mean?

TOM
No longer will we be given
minimum wage for jobs that,
granted, anyone could do.

THE BUILDERS
Yeah!

TOM
No longer will we have to
work long hours, often with
no time to take our post
lunch break.

THE BUILDERS
Yeah!

TOM
No longer will we be held
accountable for work, while
being deprived of our mid
afternoon beauty sleep.

THE BUILDERS
Yeah!

TOM
Men. Today, we will strike!

THE BUILDERS
Yeah!

>   TOM
Will you follow me?

>   THE BUILDERS
Yeah!

>   TOM
Will you follow me?

>   THE BUILDERS
Yeah!

>   TOM
Follow me now, then.

>   THE BUILDERS
Where?

>   TOM
To get haircuts.

INT. BARBERSHOP - DAY

The builders line up in seats, all getting their hair cut exactly like Tom.

Tom marches behind them.

>   TOM
You are to be my followers,
you are all to have the same
haircut.

>   THE BUILDERS
It is very, very important!

EXT. BUILDING SITE - GROUND AREA - DAY

The builders stand around with their hair cut. Tom stands in front of them.

                    TOM
          Now that we have the same
          hair cut, I will go to the
          control room, to strategize.

He stomps his foot and marches towards the portacabin.

Grace arrives in her car.

She pulls up next to the builders.

                    GRACE
          What are you doing?

                    MARK
          We're striking.

                    GRACE
          What does that mean?

                    GARY
          We're standing around,
          doing nothing until we get
          paid.

                    GRACE
          How is that different from
          what you normally do?

The builders look to one another for an answer and find none.

                    GARY
          Tom is our leader.

INT. PORTACABIN - MEETING ROOM - DAY

Tom has taken command of the portacabin.

He sits on a cushioned chair, with his feet up on a desk.

He blows cigar smoke into the air.

The smoke drifts past an oil painting on the wall.

The painting depicts Tom, topless, being licked by a bear,

Tom applies RoGain to his upper lip, just as Grace enters.

                    GRACE
          I need to speak with you.

                    TOM
          I will be the speaker around
          here.

Grace picks him up and throws him out the window.

EXT. PORTACABIN - DAY

Tom lands with a bump on his bottom.

The painting flies out of the window after him.

INT. HOUSE - DAY

Jane works on a laptop.

Tom enters carrying the painting.

                    TOM
Good news, dear. The work
resolution is underway. The
strike is initiated. Now, for
the garden!

Tom hangs the painting above the fire place.

                    JANE
Tom, please calm down.

                    TOM
Don't you get it? Their
gardens are getting bigger,
while ours are getting
smaller.

                    JANE
You've got something on
your lip.

                    TOM
I'm growing a mustache.

Jane closes the laptop.

                    JANE
That's it Tom. That's
enough. I want you to get
help.

                    TOM
It's just a bit of facial
decoration.

                    JANE
First it was the strutting, and
the hair, the clothes, tattoos,
a car we can't afford.

                    TOM
          Payment plan.

                    JANE
          You start smoking. A dog.
          What makes you think you
          can grow anything?

                    TOM
          I'm using RoGain.

                    JANE
          Oh for... that's it, I'm making
          an appointment to see
          Doctor Parker.

                    TOM
          Fine, fine. But first I will
          confront the neighbors!

He straightens his Napoleon hat.

                    JANE
          Be careful.

Tom leaves.

EXT. MELLOR STREET - HUGH AND NANCY'S HOUSE - DAY

Tom marches down the street, carrying a general's staff. He turns 90 degrees, and heads straight up to the front door of Hugh and Nancy. He knocks with his staff.

Nancy, Hugh's girlfriend, answers the door.

                    TOM
          I've got a bone to pick with
          you, Missy. Where is your
          boyfriend?

                    NANCY
          Oh, my God.
                    (calling inside)
          Which one of you sent me a
          stripper-gram.

Friends, AMBER and SINDY, appear behind Nancy.

                    AMBER
          He's so cute!

                    TOM
          You'll not get away with
          this.

                    SINDY
          He's a munchkin!

                    TOM
          You have not seen the last of
          me, you hear me?

                    NANCY
          I love midget strippers.

                    TOM
          I'll be back!

INT. DOCTORS OFFICE - DAY

Jane and Tom are back with Doctor Parker.

                    JANE
He's been acting very
strange.

                    DOCTOR
          (to Tom)
It appears your brain is
shrinking.

                    JANE
What? I don't understand.

                    DOCTOR
Let me explain.

Doctor Parker reaches over to his anatomy model and inflates an
inflatable brain.

                    DOCTOR
Take this brain. Bigger,
bigger,
there we go. Now watch
what happens
to the brain.

                    TOM
Ok.

Nothing happens.

                    DOCTOR
Watching?

                    TOM
Yes.

He pops the brain with a needle.

                              DISSOLVE TO:

<u>1 FOOT (30.48CM)</u>

INT. LIVING ROOM - DAY

An eerie quiet hangs over the living room.

The curtains are drawn.

Whatever is in there doesn't want to be seen...

Tom comes into view, walking under the table, weaving in and out of the legs of the chairs...

He's ridiculously small now. There's not much left of him.

                    TOM
          Kids, kids, where are you?

Tom looks up at the sofa.

                    TOM
          Kids, are you up there?

Tom walks over to the door.

He sticks his head through the cat flap.

EXT. GARDEN - DAY

Davy and Sarah are feral, in rags, their hair disheveled. They chase each-other round the garden on all fours.

Through the cat flap, Tom looks on in horror.

                    TOM
          Um... Kids?

The kids stop chasing each-other.

They stand upright.

INT. LIVING ROOM - DAY

Tom address Davy and Sarah - under the dining table.

>TOM
>How long did I leave you
>out there?

>DAVY
>It was quite long, Dad.

>SARAH
>We went a bit wild.

>TOM
>You did go a bit wild.

>DAVY
>We're embarrassed.

>TOM
>Anyway, this is why I called
>you in.

Tom pulls a string to reveal an aerial photograph of the neighborhood.

>TOM
>This is our street, here. And
>this is our garden, here.

>DAVY & SARAH
>Yay!

TOM

Or that's where our garden
was, because our neighbor
has been moving his fence
into our space. He's taking
our space!

DAVY & SARAH

Booo!

TOM

Exactly, boo. Your mother
doesn't seem to care.

SARAH

Booo!

TOM

So, we're going to teach
these neighbors a lesson.
We're going to show them
what happens when
someone tries to walk over
Tom Manginer!

DAVY

Are we going to kill them
and eat them?

TOM

No. We're going to bombard
them with rotten vegetables
until they surrender. Are you
with me?

DAVY

Yay!

                    TOM
Wanna go get the
vegetables?

                    SARAH
Yay!

                    TOM
And the cannon?

                    DAVY
Yay!

                    SARAH
And then can we try the
slide where you work?

                    TOM
Yep. Let's go!

EXT. GROCERY STORE - DAY

Davy and Sarah pull up outside the grocery store on their bicycles.
Tom sits in Davy's basket, shrouded in a blanket, like ET.

He throws off the blanket.

                    TOM
Fill the bags with the oldest
fruit and vegetables they've
got.

The kids dismount.

                    TOM
Go for the grapefruit. They
sting!

EXT. TENNIS STORE - DAY

The kids and Tom pull up outside the tennis store.

He throws off the blanket.

> TOM
> Cannons!

EXT. MELLOR STREET - DAY

Tom leads Davy and Sarah down Mellor Street.

> TOM
> Halt.

They stop.

> TOM
> Attention.

They stand ready.

> TOM
> Positions.

They crouch down behind tennis ball firing cannons, and load them up with rotten vegetables and grapefruit.

> TOM
> Ready, aim, fire.

BANG.

Tom, Davy and Sarah fire away at the home of Hugh and Nancy.

Vegetables and fruit splatter over the building.

INT. HUGH AND NANCY'S HOUSE - DAY

Hugh and Nancy gather at the window.

> HUGH
> What the hell are they
> doing?

> NANCY
> We're under attack. I told
> you they were coming for
> us. They want their land
> back!

> HUGH
> I'll deal with this!

EXT. HUGH AND NANCY'S HOUSE - DAY

Hugh exits the house.

He's bombarded by a barrage of fruit and vegetables.

> HUGH
> Stop. I surrender. I
> surrender.

Tom and the kids cheer.

EXT. GARDEN - DAY

Tom plants a flag in the grass of his reclaimed garden.

The flag features the image of Tom being licked by a bear.

INT. KITCHEN - DAY

Jane answers the door to Grace, who is dressed in a skimpy red dress and high heels.

                    GRACE
          Jane, I need to come in.

Grace steps in past a flustered Jane.

                    GRACE
          Jane, I happened to be in the
          neighborhood, and just had
          to stop by, are you sure you
          don't want to check each-
          other's boobs?

Tom and the kids enter, fresh from battle.

Tom goes immediately wild.

He leaps on Grace, straddling her, pulling her hair.

Grace screams.

                    JANE
          Tom, calm down.

Sarah throws Tom half a grapefruit.

He presses the grapefruit into Grace's face.

                    GRACE
          My eyes, my eyes!

Tom jumps down from Grace as she flees from the house.

                    TOM
          And that is expert parenting!

                    JANE
Tom, you're going mad.

                    TOM
I am not going mad. I am not
going mad.

A DELIVERY DRIVER cranes his head round the door.

                    DELIVERY DRIVER
Delivery's here.

EXT. TOM'S HOUSE - DAY

The DELIVERY TEAM erects a ten foot statue of Tom on the
front lawn.

INT. KITCHEN - DAY

Jane looks through the window and sees the statue going up.

                    JANE
Kids, go to your room.

                    TOM
They can stay.

                    SARAH
Should one of us stay and
one of us
go?

                    TOM
Jane?

                    JANE
Just go.

The twins run off.

>   JANE
> My patience is really being
> tested.

>   TOM
> She's only four.

>   JANE
> Have you no sense of
> responsibility whatsoever?

>   TOM
> Ah, I see what's happening
> here,
> things are looking up for
> me...

>   JANE
> No.

>   TOM
> So you get uneasy...

>   JANE
> No.

>   TOM
> Can't be happy for me...

>   JANE
> I don't like the person you've
> become.

>   TOM
> You didn't like the person I
> was before, either. And
> neither did I.

Jane storms out.

                    TOM
               (to himself)
          Fee Fi Fo Fum...

INT. KIDS BEDROOM - DAY

The twins play with the doll house.

Tom sits in the doll house dining room, at a table across from Hip-Hop Barbie, having imaginary tea.

                    DAVY
          Why aren't you sleeping in
          your
          bedroom?

                    TOM
          Because Mummy doesn't
          give me enough respect. She
          doesn't treat me seriously.

                    SARAH
               (as Hip-Hop
               Barbie)
          Would you like some more
          tea?

                    TOM
          Yes, please.

Sarah pours some more imaginary tea into Tom's toy cup.

                    TOM
          Thank you.

He takes a sip.

TOM
(to Hip-Hop
Barbie)
Will Roller Barbie be
joining us, this evening?

SARAH
(as Hip-Hop
Barbie)
I don't think so.

TOM
Shame.

Davy picks up Barbie's hair brush.

DAVY
Dad, can I brush your hair?

TOM
Yeah. Is it looking flat?

Davy picks up his Dad, cradles him in his arms, and starts to brush his hair.

TOM
Nice and big.

SARAH
Would you like some milk,
Daddy?

TOM
Sure.

Sarah puts a bowl of milk down on the floor. Davy places Tom beside the bowl. Tom begins to lap it up.

SARAH
There, there kitty kitty.

                    TOM
What? Wait a minute! What
is this?

                    SARAH
What's wrong?

                    TOM
You're treating me like a cat.

                    DAVY
You're a pussy.

                    TOM
This is demeaning. You can't
treat your father like a pet
kitten. I won't stand for it.

The twins run out of the room.

                    TOM
Kids, kids.

They've gone.

                    TOM (CONT'D)
Damn it.

INT. BEDROOM - NIGHT

The twins are in bed with Jane.

                    SARAH
You can see the stars from
your room.

                    JANE
Have you remembered to
make your wish?

> DAVY
> Yeah, shiny slide at Dad's
> work.

> SARAH
> And ice cream.

> DAVY
> Do you think Dad's brain
> will ever grow back?

> JANE
> I don't know, Davy. Go to
> sleep.

The kids turn over and go to sleep.

The sound of rustling covers comes from an adjacent room.

Jane gets up and follows the sound into the hallway.

INT. KIDS BEDROOM - NIGHT

Jane enters the room.

The light is on in the doll house.

The tapping sound comes from an upstairs doll house bedroom.

Jane peers into the doll house bedroom.

The tapping is coming from the doll house bed.

The covers are moving...

> JANE
> Hello?

Tom, in the doll house bed, pulls back the covers, red faced.

                    TOM
          It's not what it looks like.

Jane pulls the covers back further to reveal Roller Barbie.

                    JANE
          Oh my God. You're cheating
          on me with Roller Barbie.

                    TOM
          We were just talking. She
          listens to me!

EXT. HOUSE - NIGHT

The kids wait in the back of a taxi. Jane loads up the trunk.

                    SARAH
          Are we going on a trip?

                    JANE
          Yes.

                    DAVY
          Shiny slide!

                    SARAH
          That was some good
          wishing.

                    JANE
          We're going to stay with my
          friends for a little while.

                    DAVY
          Are they coming sliding,
          too?

INT. KIDS BEDROOM - DOLL HOUSE - NIGHT

Through the doll house window, and out through the bedroom window, Tom watches his family go.

INT. LIVING ROOM - DAY

Barely any light streams into the room, now.

Tom sits on the sofa, dwarfed by its size.

He sings to himself, getting weaker.

                              TOM
                         (singing)
                    They laugh at me, these
                    fellas,
                    Just because I am small
                    They laugh at me because
                    I'm not hundred feet tall!
                    I tell 'em there's a lot to learn
                    down here on the ground.
                    The world is big, but little
                    people turn it around!

                                        DISSOLVE TO:

10CM

EXT. TOM'S HOUSE - DAY

Tom bursts out of the front door, in all his ten magnificent centimeters, to greet a new day.

He's dressed again in his leather jacket and shades, and he sings, accompanied by a full orchestra, dancing past the statue of himself and over to his doll sized car.

> TOM
> (singing)
> A worm can roll a stone,
> A bee can sting a bear,
> A fly can fly around
> Versailles,
> 'Cos flies don't care,
> A sparrow in a hut,
> Can make a happy home,
> A flea can bite the bottom,
> Of the Pope in Rome.
> Goliath was a bruiser who
> was tall as the sky.
> But David threw a right and
> gave him one in the eye.
> I never read the Bible but I
> know that it's true.
> It only goes to show what
> little people can do!

Tom gets in the car and buckles the seat-belt.

> TOM
> (to himself)
> I'm going to drink myself to
> death.

Tom's poodle runs out of the house and into the garden.

It begins to pee on the statue.

                    TOM
          Goodbye house. Goodbye
          statue. Goodbye ludicrous
          dog.

The statue moves slightly.

Tom starts the car.

The statue moves again, and Tom notices.

Despite being massive, the statue is being moved by the poodle's
seemingly endless stream of pee, and it moves in the direction of
Tom in his car.

                    TOM
          Careful, Pitbull. It's insecure.

The dog continues to pee.

The statue continues to move.

                    TOM
          It's insecure, Pitbull. It's
          insecure.

The statue is clearly going to topple in Tom's direction.

Tom tries to unbuckle his seatbelt.

It's stuck.

Tom wrestles with it, but it's no use.

                    TOM
          Insecure! Insecure! Insecure!

The statue crashes down on Tom's car...

Just as Tom dives to safety.

Tom sits up on the garden lawn and surveys the carnage.

His car is crushed.

The head of the statue has smashed through the kitchen window and the front wall of the house.

                    TOM
          I wasn't secure.

INT. THE MORNING SUN BAR - DAY

Tom sits on a stool alongside Ex Chief Supervisor Jones.

The barman serves two beers. Tom's beer is in a thimble.

                    TOM
          It's a revelation. The reason I
          did all of this. The hair, the
          clothes, even the tattoos - I
          was insecure.

                    JONES
          Hmmm... You know, that's
          maybe why I drink the way I
          do.

                    TOM
          Why didn't I admit it? Why
          didn't I just say, I feel
          insecure? Why act out with
          all that effort, that time?

                    JONES
               (to the
               Barman)
          You know what? I'll just
          have a juice.

                    TOM
          I've got to tell the guys.

EXT. BUILDING SITE - GROUND AREA -

Tom stands in front of his builder team.

                    TOM
          Men, I have something
          important I want to say to
          you.

He removes his sunglasses.

                    TOM
          Recently, you may have
          noticed me acting strange
          around here.

                    BUILDERS
          No, no, not at all.

                    TOM
          It's ok. I admit it. The
          shouting, the posing, the
          ordering. Getting you all to
          follow my haircut. The ab
          implants.

                    GARY
          We didn't know you had ab
          implants.

TOM

I perhaps didn't mention it.
But the point is, instead of
all this acting out, I wish I
had just said, men, I feel
insecure. I feel insecure
because I'm small.

BUILDERS

No, no, you're not.

TOM

It's ok. I am small. And
that's ok. And it's ok to feel
insecure, right? It's ok not to
be perfect.

The men digest this.

TOM

What's not ok, is to spend all
of our lives trying to hide it!

GARY

I... I feel insecure
sometimes, because I'm
worried some of the other
fellas will realize I'm gay.

OTHER BUILDERS

It's ok. It's ok.

GARY

That's why I grew this beard.

OTHER BUILDERS

We knew you were gay.

The builders pat Gary on the back, reassuringly.

MARK

I feel insecure because my
beard is not as long as Gary's
beard!

OTHER BUILDERS

It's ok. It's ok.

MARK

I don't even like beards.

TOM

See what I mean?

MARK

The hours I spend grooming!

STEVE

I feel insecure because my
parents disowned me; they
wanted a girl.

OTHER BUILDERS

All our parents wanted girls!

Everyone hugs Steve.

TOM

We can't waste any more
time and effort hiding our
insecurities.

BUILDERS

Yeah!

TOM

Just admit them, and move
on. It's getting in the way of
our lives, our relationships,
our work.

GARY
Does that mean we can get
back to work?

TOM
You can get back to work,
and you can have any
hairstyle and facial hair you
want.

BUILDERS
Yeah!

MARK
I'm dying to shave!

INT. BIG BOSS'S CAR - DAY

The car approaches the building site, with The Big Boss and Grace
seated in the back.

GRACE
They just refuse to work.
They're striking. Manginer's
behind this. They should all
be fired.

EXT. BUILDING SITE - DAY

The Big Boss and Grace exit the car.

The building site is a hive of activity.

Gary, Mark, Steve and the whole team, bustle to and fro.

Girders rise through the air.

Vehicles heave soil.

Builders high five as they get on with their work.

At ground level, Tom oversees everything.

                    BIG BOSS
          Well, well.

                    GRACE
          I, I, I...

The Big Boss approaches Tom.

                    BIG BOSS
          Quite a team you've got
          here, Tom.

                    TOM
          Well, they're good people.
          We just had to clear some
          layers, first.

                    BIG BOSS
          I see.

                    GARY
             (to Tom)
          Boss, we'll have this turned
          around by sunrise.

                    GRACE
          I, I, I...

                    BIG BOSS
          Tom, I'd like to promote you
          to Chief Supervisor, taking
          this project to completion.
          You think you can handle a
          responsibility of that size?

                    TOM
     I can handle it. I'm big
     enough.

INT. HUGH AND NANCY'S HOUSE - DAY

Nancy gives a sick looking Hugh a head message.

The bell rings.

Hugh lets out a shriek.

                    NANCY
     Calm down. Calm down.

Nancy heads over to the front door. Hugh cowers behind.

They answer the door to a confident, casually dressed Tom.

He's grown - to around one foot - 30.48cm.

                    HUGH
     Eeek!

                    TOM
     Hello, Hugh, Nancy. I just
     wanted to apologize for my
     behavior. While I won't
     allow anyone to take
     anything which is rightfully
     mine, I shouldn't have
     bombarded you with rotten
     vegetables. And grapefruit.

                    NANCY
     Thank you.

                    TOM
     It won't happen again.

Tom makes to leave.

> TOM
> Hugh, return my lawn
> mower.

He's gone.

> HUGH
> I hate that man.

> NANCY
> Oh, I don't know. I think he's
> kind of cute.

INT. TOM'S HOUSE - DAY

Tom orchestrates a complete renovation of his home while performing a musical number.

Gary, Mark, Steve and Ex Chief Supervisor Jones help him.

They each boast their own identity and style, now.

They're individual people.

Tom removes the painting of himself from the wall.

> TOM
> (singing)
> A worm can roll a stone,
> A bee can sting a bear,
> A fly can fly around
> Versailles,
> 'Cos flies don't care,
> A sparrow in a hut,
> Can make a happy home,
> A flea can bite the bottom,
> Of the Pope in Rome,

So listen here professor,
With your head in the cloud.
It's often kind of useful,
To get lost in the crowd.
So keep your universities,
I don't give a damn,
For better or for worse it is,
The way that I am!

Tom guides Gary and Mark in the creation of a porch with a sitting swing in the front garden.

BUILDERS CHORUS
(singing)
Be careful where you go
'Cos little people grow...
And little people know,
When little people fight,
They may look easy
pickings but they got some
bite!
So never kick a dog because
he's just a pup,
You better run for cover
when the pup grows up!

TOM
(singing)
And we'll fight like twenty
armies,
And we won't give up.

Tom oversees the creation of a conservatory in the garden.

TOM
(singing)
A worm can roll a stone,
A bee can sting a bear,

A fly can fly around
Versailles,
'Cos flies don't care,
A sparrow in a hut,
Can make a happy home,
A flea can bite the bottom,
Of the Pope in Rome.

At the front of the house, as the music plays out, Tom waves
goodbye to the builders as they drive away, dragging the statue
behind them.

                    TOM
              (singing -
              baritone)
         A flea can bite the bottom,
         Of the Pope in Rome.

He closes the door.

                              DISSOLVE TO:

<u>2 FOOT 2 (66CM)</u>

INT. LIVING ROOM - DAY

Tom enters his newly renovated living room. The space is bright and airy.

He sits down on the sofa and exhales a contented sigh.

All is well.

Then his eyes go wide as he remembers.

                    TOM
          My family!

EXT. TOM'S HOUSE - DAY

Tom bursts out of the house.

He surveys the front garden: crushed car, poodle on the lawn.

Tom disappears round the driveway and returns with one of the twins' scooters.

He brings it to the poodle.

                    TOM
          Track, Pitbull, track.

EXT. MOTORWAY - DAY

Pitbull the poodle pulls Tom, on the scooter.

They weave in and out of traffic.

TOM
Good, Pitbull, good.

EXT. TOY STORE - DAY

Pitbull pulls Tom past the toy store.

They keep going.

EXT. GROCERY STORE - DAY

Pitbull pulls Tom past the grocery store.

They keep going.

EXT. THE MORNING SUN BAR - DAY

Pitbull pulls Tom past the now boarded up bar.

They keep going.

EXT. JANE'S FRIENDS' HOUSE - DAY

An un-kept garden leads to a un-kept house.

The sounds of Justin Beiber squeak from inside.

INT. LIVING ROOM - JANE'S FRIENDS' HOUSE - DAY

Becky, Anne and Claire lounge around the room in onesies.

The layers of glamour with which they bury themselves when they leave the house are absent.

Here, the women live like regressed students.

Posters of pop stars line the walls.

Empty snack packets litter the floor.

Jane enters from the garden.

                    JANE
          The kids are playing outside.
          I'm going to stay in my room
          for a little while.

The friends don't look up from their phones.

                    JANE
          We really do appreciate you
          letting us stay here.

The friends remain in social media zone, oblivious.

EXT. JANE'S FRIENDS' HOUSE - DAY

Tom pulls up on the scooter.

He releases Pitbull.

                    TOM
          Well done, Pitbull.

Tom looks up at the house.

He sees Jane moving around in the upstairs bedroom.

                    TOM
          Jane.

Tom runs up to the front door.

He can't reach the door bell.

Surveying the house, Tom spots a drain pipe leading up the side of the building, and over the upstairs bedroom.

Tom climbs the drain-pipe.

INT. JANE'S ROOM - DAY

Jane lies on the bed, drowning tears into the pillow.

There's a little tap on the window.

Jane looks up to see Tom, perched on the window ledge.

                    JANE
          Tom!

She lets him in, and hugs him.

Then she drops him.

                    TOM
          Ow!

                    JANE
          I'm still angry with you.

                    TOM
          You should be. I've been a
          fool.

Jane sits down on the bed.

Tom climbs up and sits beside her.

                    TOM
          How are you, Jane?

JANE
I hate it here. It's not a
healthy environment for me,
for the kids.

TOM
I'm sorry, Jane.

JANE
It's not just you. It's both of
us. What happened?

TOM
I just stopped trying. I
stopped speaking up. I don't
know why.

JANE
Was it me?

TOM
No, I think I was just
overwhelmed with family
and work. I hadn't prepared
myself for it. I just let it take
over me.

JANE
You weren't like this when
we met.

TOM
I know. I don't know when it
started. Maybe I let one
dream go, then another day
go, without speaking up,
without taking action.

JANE
I just saw you drift away.

TOM
The problem was there long
before I started shrinking.

JANE
I love you, Tom.

TOM
I love you, too.

They hug.

JANE
You're growing.

TOM
Really? I extended the
house.

JANE
But don't you realize, I don't
care how big you are, or
how big the house is. I love
you. I just wanted you to
realize that. I wanted you to
care about yourself.

TOM
I know.

JANE
Taking care of your family
doesn't mean not taking care
of yourself.

TOM
Can I see the kids?

                    JANE
          They miss you. They're in
          the garden.

EXT. GARDEN - DAY

Tom and Jane enter the garden.

The kids are missing.

                    TOM
          Where are they?

                    JANE
          I don't understand it. They
          were here a minute a go.

                    TOM
          Jane!

                    JANE
          They were asking about you.
          Saying you were going to
          take them on a shiny slide.

                    TOM
          Oh, God. I know where they
          are!

EXT. BUILDING SITE - DAY

The site bustles with activity.

Tom and Jane arrive in a taxi.

Tom immediately looks up at the shiny garbage chute, descending
from the higher floors into a skip.

EXT. BUILDING SITE - CHUTE ENTRANCE - DAY

With a backdrop of clouds, blue sky and fresh air, Davy and Sarah climb into the chute.

> DAVY
>
> Shiny slide!

> SARAH
>
> Me first.

> DAVY
>
> No, me first.

They climb in together.

It is at this moment that the sheer height of the chute becomes apparent to Davy and Sarah, and the inevitable result of them descending at an almost vertical angle becomes clear.

> SARAH
>
> I don't want to do it.

> DAVY
>
> Me neither.

It's too late.

They turn to climb out of the chute, but they've gone too far.

They slip, and barely stop themselves from falling by holding to the inner rim of the chute.

Their screams echo down into the darkness of the metal.

At the end of the girder, along from the chute entrance, Tom appears, stepping off a crate, attached to a wooden pulley.

> TOM
>
> Kids!

Tom makes his way gingerly along the girder. His tiny frame is blown by the wind in this upper reach of the construction.

                    TOM
          I'm coming, kids. Hold on!

EXT. BUILDING SITE - GROUND AREA - DAY

Jane, Gary, Mark and Steve gather round as the whole site comes to a halt.

They watch as Tom makes his way along the upper girder, and they let out a collective gasp as Tom slips.

EXT. BUILDING SITE - CHUTE ENTRANCE - DAY

Tom regains his footing and holds on to the chute.

He peers in.

                DAVY & SARAH
          Daddy!

                    TOM
          Take my hands, kids!

Sarah grabs Tom's hands.

                   SARAH
          Help me, Daddy!

Tom tries to lift with his all his might, but he can't lift the weight.

                    TOM
          I can't, I can't.

                   DAVY
          Daddy, I'm slipping.

                    TOM
          I'm sorry, kids.

                   SARAH
          Daddy!

Tom places Sarah's hands back on the rim of the chute.

He looks Davy and Sarah in the eye.

                    TOM
          You're going to be ok.

Tom climbs into the chute with his kids.

                   SARAH
          Daddy, what are you doing?

                    TOM
          I'm just not strong enough to
          lift you at this moment. And
          I'm ok with admitting that.
          We're going to slide down
          together, kids. You're going
          to land on me.

EXT. BUILDING SITE - GROUND AREA - DAY

The crowd gasps as Tom climbs into the chute.

Jane's eyes well up with tears.

EXT. BUILDING SITE - CHUTE ENTRANCE - DAY

Tom, Davy and Sarah hang from the chute entrance.

Tom lowers himself, holding on by a finger, so that he's slightly
below his two children.

TOM
This is it, kids. Ready?

DAVY AND SARAH
Ready.

TOM
I love you, kids. Let go.

Tom and his children let go of the chute.

The children fall into Tom, descending into the darkness of the chute, leaving a trail of screams.

EXT. BUILDING SITE - GROUND AREA - DAY

Members of the crowd gasp, shield their eyes and turn away as the sound of the descending objects rattles through the metallic chute.

In a collective blur, Tom, Davy and Sarah fly out the end of the chute and crash into the skip.

Dust rises in their wake.

Jane runs up to the skip.

A silence descends upon the building site.

Davy and Sarah stand up from the depths of the skip, alive.

The crowd cheers.

Davy and Sarah allow sheepish grins to spread across their faces.

And Tom stands up beside them, bruised and battered, but bigger.

He's 3 FOOT 11 (119.38CM).

DAVY & SARAH
Can we do that, again?

Tom thinks about it for a second.

TOM

Yeah, ok.

Danger zone.

FADE TO BLACK.

THE END

ALSO AVAILABLE

WOMEN ON TOP: A DUD'S TALE

In a utopian near future, women run the world, and they have finally sorted it out.

Nurturing the earth back to health following centuries of male violence, and creating a pristine commercial paradise, women have separated men into those that are fertile, Studs, and those that are useless, Duds.

It is one such Dud, he who is labelled Wimpole, who threatens this paradise. Mistakenly assigned as a Stud through a (male) clerical error, and assigned to impregnate the noble Commandress Roseanne, Dud Wimpole threatens the very fabric of our ideal future society.

It is the account of Dud Wimpole that is presented here, *A Dud's Tale*, discovered by a present day Primary school teacher, highlighting the dangers of allowing men to read and write, and reminding us all why they should not be allowed anywhere near Primary schools.

WOMEN ON TOP 2: THE TESTICLES

He may be mankind's last hope, but how long can hope last?

Dud Wimpole puts on the fake moustache one last time in a call to action that even he can't ignore.

What follows is a descent from freedom to entrapment, calm to chaos and coconut trees to reality TV...

Chronicled through the testaments of three eye witnesses, *Women on Top 2: The Testicles* provides a well-rounded portrait of a very scrawny man.

Presented in the famed EB Garamond font with an Introduction by Professor Games Cevin Cleftbottom, Rutherford College.

PRISON BREAK!

From the creators of *ODD*, it's time to take a *Prison Break!*

Struggling with life on the outside, three disenfranchised, emasculated males decide to escape by breaking into prison.

It was the most secure prison in the world, but they were determined to break in.

The feature length screenplay.

162

ODD

When a pandemic of Oppositional Defiant Disorder afflicts the male population of the world, women must work together to save humanity. It's a disaster movie.

In the first quarter of the year 2022, the motion picture, *ODD*, was filmed with an estimated budget of $240 million.

The film was screened once, at the Westwood Village Theatre in Los Angeles.

Following the screening, the single known print of the movie was burned at the request of the studio.

This is the screenplay.

THE ANKLE PROBLEM

What is the problem?

Marcus seems to have it all, a great job, a nice house and a good bunch of friends he plays football with at the weekends.

Plus he's married his beloved Amy, and they've just got back from their honeymoon.

But in the weeks after the marriage, nobody sees Marcus. No friends, no football, no Marcus. He says he has an ankle problem, but can this be the whole story?

How did he injure his ankle while on honeymoon?

How does his ankle prevent him from going out for a drink?

And what's that unearthly sound of something cracking coming from his house?

It turns out, Marcus may have a bigger problem than his ankle.

A horror screenplay from the writers of *Women on Top: A Dud's Tale* and *Prison Break!*

Part of the *Modern Fables* series.

166

AUTHENTICITY

Craig Curelip, 25, lives by an "own everything, use nothing"
philosophy. He hopes that his extreme frugality will allow
him to retire by the time he's 28.

For most 25-year-olds, retirement practically could not seem
further away. That is not the case for Craig Curelip.
Curelip, who lives in Denver in the US state of Colorado, is
a member of the increasingly popular FIRE movement
(financial
independence, retire early).

Followers of the philosophy live by a minimalist, frugal
lifestyle enabling them to save as much money as possible to
retire as early as they are able. In Curelip's case, the
target age is 28.

His "own everything, use nothing" philosophy" has touched
nearly every corner of his existence, augmenting the way he
lives. He has even gone so far as renting out his bedroom and
sleeping in his living room for a year.

A financial advisor by trade, Curelip feels that with his
strategies to save, and determination to be able to quit his
salaried job, by 28 he will "definitely be there…

This is the story of what happens when Craig meets a
stripper.

Part of the *Modern Fables* series.

VOTE LIAM!

A sociopathic, alcoholic ex-con decides to make a difference to the village which shunned him by running for mayor.

A full-length screenplay.

Part of the *Modern Fables* series.

UNDER THE SOFA

The multiverse has its first hero, and his name is Bernard.

Theorising that there was a black hole in his living room, Bernard Hobbs crawled under his sofa, and vanished...

He awoke to find himself in distant worlds, alike our own, but worse, and pursued by a man from the tax office, to which he owes 12p.

And so, Mr. Hobbs finds himself escaping from world to world, anxious that his 12p debt is accruing interest, desperate not to incur the wrath of his wife, and hoping each time that his next escape, will be the escape home.

Collected together in this limited edition, the teleplays from the complete first series.

SMALL MAN COMPLEX

NOBLES: THE MUSICAL

In the tradition of *Bartleby, the Scrivener*, *Down and Out in Paris and London* and *Man of La Mancha*, comes *Nobles: The Musical!*

The post-pandemic world has seen a reluctance amongst the workforce to return to work.

Schemes such as furlough, government subsidies and work-from-home have made non-engagement in work the norm.

Coupled with this is the perhaps tone deaf, multi-million pound coronation of King Charles III, unprecedented profits for supermarkets and energy companies monopolising essential services, and cultural emphasis on personal wellbeing.

However, for a group of friends in one seafront arcade coffee shop, the life of non-work is nothing new.

Using an expert knowledge of the UK welfare system, a philosophical adherence to non-participation and a carefully cultivated lack of skills, the Nobles have managed to avoid work for going on half a century.

And tonight, they're going to sing about it.

WOMEN ON TOP: FREESOME

Dud Wimpole has vanished…

The former star of Dileag's cultural phenomenon, *Keeping Up With the Commandresses*, leaves behind an extremist right-wing female led republic rocked by the escape of its most infamous male-inadequate. Its fascist structure, built around separating fertile men into Studs and infertile men into Duds, has started to crack.

On the other side of the country, the extremist left-wing, female led city-state San Francesca is trying not to notice. Suspected of harbouring the child that Dud Wimpole helped escape Dileag years before, known in lore as Baby Dud, San Francesca minds its own business, resisting any engagement with its distant neighbour, and content in its own policy of "worst is best."

But some things can't be ignored. Some forces, once awoken, can not be stopped: the march of time, the call of fate, the inevitability of war…

The battle for the future begins tonight.

"This is the Real Deal. A story of war and women, men and moustaches, boys and balls, girls and guns… A lost son takes his rightful place at the seat of society, at the end of history, at the dawn of the future… This is epic stuff. A must read." Kamala Harris

COMING SOON

STORIES TO READ ON THE TRAIN

All aboard!

A collection of short stories to read on the train, designed to match the rhythms of the great locomotives, short enough to enjoy between stations, long enough to immerse the reader in a momentary escape into the lives and concerns of others.

Some of these stories may raise a chuckle from the reader which melds with the chuffa-chuffa, chuffa-chuffa of their carriages. For those of you no longer riding steam engines, you get the picture.

A notable fact: those of you on the journey from London to Brighton on the non-express service will notice that these stories have been presented to fill the space between stations on the route quite perfectly, assuming one has the normal reading age/speed of an average small adult.

Attention: This book has been delayed due to leaves on the track.

182

183

184